Kathle

Healing and
Wholeness

Prayers, reflections, and rituals
for those who are ill or dying

First published in 2009 by
the columba press
55a Spruce Avenue, Stillorgan Industrial Park, Blackrock, Co Dublin

Designed by Bill Bolger
Illustrated by Emer O'Boyle
Music typeset by Matthew Hébert
Origination by The Columba Press
Printed in Ireland by ColourBooks Ltd, Dublin

ISBN 978 1 85607 674 6

Acknowledgements
The author and publisher are grateful to the following for permission to quote from works in their copyright: Sorin Books, Notre Dame, Indiana for two quotations from *Radical Amazement* by Judy Cannato; Barnes and Noble for a quotation from *On Life After Death* by Elizabeth Kübler-Ross; Crossroad Publishing Company for a quotation from *Here and Now: Living in the Spirit* by Henri Nouwen; Mary T. Malone for two quotations from her *Praying with the Women Mystics*.

Table of Contents

In loving memory of
Cecelia Guckian RSM
Kathleen McQuaid RSM
Maura O Dowd

Introduction

Family and friends sat around Cecelia's bed in the Hospice in Sligo searching for a common language in which to pray. Her niece, Rhona, turned to me and said, 'Kathleen, why don't you write a book of simple prayers in contemporary language for occasions such as this?' The seed of the book was sown.

Writing, however, was put on the long finger. A year afterwards another good friend of mine, Kathleen, lay dying in the Hospice in Tullamore. Again the need for communal prayers in everyday language was evident.

When a third friend, Maura, fell ill of cancer she asked me to accompany her in her illness. Together we listened to healing chants, blessed each other with healing blessings, and celebrated healing rituals. Maura enjoyed two years of good health. Unfortunately, her cancer recurred. She asked me to lead the rituals of her wake and burial. I agreed on condition that we compose the rituals together.

After Maura's death I began to work on the book and was more than half way through when I, myself, was diagnosed with breast-cancer, had a mastectomy, and underwent chemotherapy and radio-therapy. I was fortunate to have a community, a family and close friends who loved me back to health. The caring attention of the Cancer Care Staff in the local hospital was a great support in my healing. I was blessed too to live in Sligo, a place of great natural beauty. 'Nature never did betray the heart that loved her': nature restored and healed me.

When I returned to the book I did so with a different perspective. I noticed that I was unconsciously focusing more on being restored to health than on dying so I changed the subtitle from *for the Sick and Dying* to *for the Sick or Dying*.

During my illness the following Native American verse was a source of inspiration to me:
    – Healthy feet
    Can hear the heart
    Of Holy Earth –
I pray that those who use this book will hear the heartbeat of Holy Earth, and pulsate with the energy of the Creative One who calls all to health and wholeness.

How to use this book

This book is intended for those who are ill or for those who are dying and for their carers. It provides a variety of resource material for both groups. It is a book that can be dipped into rather than one to be followed sequentially. It covers a variety of prayer forms to suit the diverse needs of users.

Chants
A free download of nine chants and eight short meditations is available on The Columba Press website, www.columba.ie. The chants can be used in a variety of ways: they can be chanted, listened to, or used in ritual.

Blessings
Blessings are an intrinsic part of Celtic life. The blessings offered are either old Celtic blessings or ones that are Celtic in nature.

Prayers
A selection of prayers is offered. These can be adapted to individual needs.

Litanies
Litanies provide a way of praying that is repetitious. They are often an easy form of prayer for a friend to use: the sick person can pray the responses with little effort.

Psalm Prayers
The psalms contained in the book express sentiments experienced in illness. They can be prayed by the sick person, by a friend, or by a group.

Meditations
There are eight meditations on the download mentioned above. You may need to pause the sound from time to time in order to facilitate contemplation. The meditations may also be led by a friend.

Rituals in sickness
The rituals offered are simple and short. They can be celebrated with another person or privately.

Rituals around death
It is envisaged that the leader of these rituals be a family member or friend. The rituals may be adapted to suit the circumstances. Together with the material offered, I recommend that you use prayers that are dear to the dying person.

Acknowledgements

Many streams flowed into the river which is this book. To each tributary I am grateful.

A major tributary was the team who composed, sang, read and produced the Download: Máirín Ní Mhurchú and Margo Lombard (melodies), Una Purcell, Nora Keenan, Ciaran McGovern, Máirín Ní Mhurchú (vocals), Celia Dunleavy (reader), and Paul Gurney (producer). Underscoring of meditations is by Paul Gurney, and arrangements by Máirín Ní Mhurchú and Paul Gurney. I owe each of them a debt of gratitude.

I am grateful, too, for the flow of inspiration and encouragement from my community, my family and friends. Kathleen Conneally read and re-read the contents. Her very helpful suggestions ripple throughout the water. Go raibh maith agat, a Chaitlín!

Sincere thanks to Seán O Boyle (The Columba Press) whose support kept the river moving with fluency, and to Bill Bolger and Emer O'Boyle who shaped its contour into a pleasing pattern.

Thanks especially to the Sisters of Mercy, Western Province, the bedrock, for allowing me the time and space for writing, and to earth for sustaining the ebb and flow of our existence.

Prayers/Reflections
in a time of illness

Life is a mystery,
Shrouded in darkness.
But the darkness is fecund,
A place of possibility and power.
What is radically amazing is that
We are invited into the darkness,
Into the heart of creation and creativity,
Invited to participate
– unsure,
But confident
In the invitation
And in the One who extends it.

Judy Cannato, *Radical Amazement*

Morning prayer

O, first rays of dawn
arising in the east
I greet you!
Birds begin to sing;
flowers are opening;
leaves are stirring;
earth awakens and
breathes forth freshness.
Awaken in me the wonder
of this new day.
Awaken in me
an openness to the possibilities
hidden in my illness.
Awaken in me
the desire to live this day
fully and vibrantly,
joyfully and peacefully,
in love and in amazement!

Prayer for Renewal

All creation is in a state of transformation,
without our conscious knowing.
As day breaks each morning
the world is renewed, refreshed,
everything is new and different,
cells in our bodies have been changed in the night.

You are the Resurrection and the Life.
You are the Transformer of the seasons.
You are the Energy of renewal.

You say: 'Behold I am making all things new.'
I am painfully aware that there are areas in me
where newness is not visible,
where renewal has not yet arrived,
where transformation is not evident.
Release within me the energy of renewal.
Transform all that is not well within.
Lead me gently during this transition
to restoration and health.

Reflection on Healing

Turner of springtime,
awaken in me a deep trust
in my body's ability to heal itself.

May I co-operate with the healing process
by eating wholesome food,
taking sufficient rest,
and exercising daily.

May I fill my being
with positive thoughts
and surround myself
with wholesome, fun-loving people.

Attuned to the natural rhythm of renewal,
I will, with patience and with faith,
await the return
of full health and happiness.

Prayer for Peace and Healing

First rays of dawn,
teach me your song of hope
that I may believe
in regeneration and renewal.

Birds of the air,
teach me the secret of your flight
that in my illness I may learn
to soar above my limitations.

Flowers of the field,
teach me the essence of your beauty
that in my illness I may come to know
the splendour of my inner beauty.

Herbs of the garden,
teach me the properties of your healing
that I may learn how to restore
my body to full health.

Mighty oak,
teach me the mystery of your growth
that I may trust in
the unfolding of my being.

Silent rock,
teach me the quality of your stillness
that I may learn to relax my body
and calm my spirit.

Flowing water,
teach me the nature of your fluidity
that I may learn to adjust
to my new circumstances.

Living earth,
teach me the depth of your riches
that I may be grounded
in your wholesomeness.

Weaving Prayer

I weave into my illness today
the healing properties of herbs.
I weave into my pain today
the eternal hope of a rainbow's arc.
I weave into my sorrow today
the joyful music of the dawn chorus.
I weave into my soul today
the deep refreshment of a gentle rain.

Prayer when I am unable to pray

When I am unable to pray help me to realise:
that the humming of a thousand bees resounds within me,
that the laughter of a thousand children sings within me,
that the dance of a thousand dolphins plays within me,
that the song of a thousand larks thrills within me,
that all creation celebrates and prays in me.
I do not need to pray.
I need to listen: creation sings my song of praise.

In times of anger

Today I identify with the energy of the volcano.
I am red hot with anger.
Why should this happen to me?
It is difficult to believe in a loving God when
every fibre of my being is burning with deep resentment
at the injustice of my illness.
I boil with rage at this pain, this illness, this suffering.
Help me to see that anger is the spark that ignites
    creativity;
that anger is the raw material for growth.
The volcano eventually cools and new life emerges from
    its fertile ashes.
May the burning of my rage make way for new growth
    in my life.
Help me to see how necessary my anger is in birthing
    newness,
in ridding myself of unhelpful emotions, in allowing me
    to move on.
God of fiery things, be with me in my rage
and lead me gently to cool waters and healing springs.

In times of fear

Today I am frozen in fear:
my body is rigid with tension.
Release within me your transforming energies:
love to soften my frozen state,
peace to loosen the grip of fear,
hope to lighten the burden of my illness.
God of the iceberg and of the thaw,
be in me the warmth of spring!

In times of anguish

'My soul is sorrowful even unto death.'
I am in anguish and distress.
Darkness envelops me,
words of comfort are empty,
my faith in a loving God shattered,
I feel abandoned.
Awaken in me the conviction that
the hour of greatest darkness
is the hour before dawn breaks.
How I long for the first rays
to appear on the horizon.

In times of pain

Today my body feels as though it is on a rack,
stretched, pulled and drawn.
Help me to see that my pain is part of the
    greater pain of the world –
the pain of sullied water,
the pain of polluted air,
the pain of depleted soil,
the pain of dying species.
Help me to accept my share of pain
without self-pity or blame.

For Self-forgiveness

Today I am overcome with a sense of failure.
I am painfully aware of dreams not fulfilled,
of ambitions not realised, of work left unfinished,
of people not cared for, of bridges not mended,
of promises not kept.
I feel that I have wasted the days of my years.

Awaken within me an acceptance of myself as I am.
Quieten the voice of excessive self criticism within me.
Awaken in me a forgiveness that is unconditional.
Lead me to the conviction that:
in you all is forgiven,
in you all is understood and accepted,
in you the prodigal is welcomed home.

Prayer of thanksgiving

This prayer is also a chant – refer to the Download

For those who walk the road with me,
lovers, dreamers, family,
I raise my heart in gratitude.
Raise your hands/arms in praise if you are able

For tears and pain transforming me,
for care and love sustaining me,
I raise my heart in gratitude.
Raise your hands/arms in praise if you are able

For splendour waiting in each seed,
for wonder winking in each weed,
I raise my heart in gratitude.
Raise your hands/arms in praise if you are able

For trust

O loving source of all that is,
you are the mother who births us,
you are the father who cradles us,
you are the lover who embraces us,
you are the friend who sustains us,
you are the one in whom we live,
and move and have our being!
O Loving Source of all that is,
be to me in my illness
mother, father, lover, and friend!

For a sense of humour

> O Divine Laughter
> echoing through the vaults of time,
> release within me the chuckle of your wit.
> Help me to know joy in the midst of suffering.
> Help me to see humour in the most unlikely places.
> Help me to poke fun at my disability,
> and to laugh kindly at the foibles of others.

For wisdom

O great spirit of wisdom, Sophia, Mother,
you who are more beautiful than life itself,
you who are the fiery power that kindles every spark,
and who breathes life into all so that nothing dies.
It is you whom I have loved and searched for from my youth.
Be with me now in my suffering,
lead me on paths of healing and happiness.
Take my hand at the moment of death
and gather me into your splendour.
Based on The Book of Wisdom, chapter 7

2/2085774

For beauty

Kindler of the night sky,
kindle your beauty within me.
May I shine with its splendour.
May I glow with its grace.
May I sparkle with its grandeur.
May I live beautifully
and die beautifully
without fear,
secure in your embrace.

For grace in difficult times

When my outward form becomes weak and feeble
may the beauty of my inner being shine through.
When I am no longer able to take care of myself
may I be gracious in accepting help from those around me.
When I am confined to bed
may I be appreciative of the care and attention of others;
may I be gracious in dependence
and respond to invasion of my privacy with grace;
may I bear indignities with courtesy,
and deflect insensitivity with humour.
May all who care for me
be blessed with health and happiness.

St Patrick's Breastplate

This is an old prayer for protection which is familiar to those within the Christian tradition. For those not in this tradition the word God or Creator can be substituted for Christ.

Christ beside me,
Christ before me,
Christ behind me,
Christ above me,
Christ below me,
Christ on my right,
Christ on my left,
Christ when I lie down,
Christ when I sit down,
Christ when I arise,
Christ in the heart of every one
Who thinks of me,
Christ in the mouth of every one
Who speaks to me,
Christ in every eye that sees me,
Christ in every ear that hears me.

Prayer of thanksgiving for illness

God, I am grateful to you
that in your mysterious love
you have taken away from me
all earthly wealth,
and that you now clothe and feed me
through the kindness of others.

God, I am grateful to you
that since you have taken away from me
the sight of my eyes
you care for me now
through the eyes of others.

God, I am grateful to you
that since you have taken away from me
the strength of my hands and heart,
you care for me now
through the hands and hearts of others.

God, I pray for them,
that you will reward them in your love,
that they may continue to love and care
until they come to a happy end
in eternity with you.

Mechthild of Magdeburg

Prayers during Chemotherapy/Radiotherapy

This is my broken body
full of metallic substances:
my mouth on fire with ulcers,
my feet blistered,
my body covered in rash,
my face distorted and swollen,
my hair in tufts on my pillow.
Barely able to lift my head,
I am nauseous and in pain.
This is my broken body!

This is my broken spirit
full of fear and dread.
I pace the floor
in the lonely hours of the long night.
My eyes are sore from weeping.
I am humiliated, misunderstood,
depressed, and alone.
This is my broken spirit.

Where do I turn in my brokenness?
Ancestors, come to my aid.
Angels, carry me.
Earth, ground me.
Water, bless me.
Fire, enliven me.
Air, in-spirit me.
Family and friends,
touch tenderly
my brokenness.

With your love only
On Download

With your love only can I face the pain,
with your love only.
With your strength only can I face the pain,
with your strength only.
With your care only can I face the pain,
with your care only.
With your hope only can I face the pain,
with your hope only.
With your faith only can I face the pain,
with your faith only.

Peace prayer at night time

Ocean of Peace,
you are the calm waters
in whose tranquillity I bathe.
You are the gentle waves
on whose crest I rest.
You are the silence of the deep
in whose serenity I sleep.
Fill me with your peace.
Hold me gently in your embrace.

Night prayer

Spirit of sleep,
bring peace and rest to my weary body.
Release me from the cares and worries of the day.
Ease my aches and pains.
Refresh my dreams.
Nourish my vision.
Gather me inward into the house of slumber
and the forgetfulness of sleep
where the seeds of renewal
and re-creation are nourished.
Amen.

Prayers for a happy death

Death is simply a shedding of the physical body
like the butterfly shedding its cocoon.
It is a transition
to a higher state of consciousness
where you continue
to perceive,
to understand,
to laugh,
and to be able to grow.

Dr Elizabeth Kübler-Ross

Celtic prayers for a happy death

God Source of All

You are the beacon that beckons us home!
You are the magnet that lures us into you!
You are the incoming tide that gathers all in your embrace!

Heartbeat of the Universe

O Gracious Creative One,
attune me to the rhythm of your heartbeat
within me,
and release in me a desire
to move gracefully
to the next stage of my journey
into a future full of promise!

Love of my life

Love of my life,
I am in you.
You are in me.
In you I live.
In you I die.
In you I dance forever.

God: Ebb and flow of the tide

From the flowing of the tide
to its ebbing,
from the waxing of the moon
to its waning,
may your love be in me/us,
may your joy enfold me/us,
may your peace sustain me/us,
may your power inflame me/us.

God be in my ebbing.
God be in my flowing.
God be present around every bend.
God be with me at journey's end.

For a conscious death

I pray that I may live with eyes wide open
to your presence in the events of each day.
I pray that I may live with ears wide open
to the song which you sing in creation.
I pray that I may live with heart wide open
to the love which pulsates in all things.

I pray that I may die with eyes wide open
to the adventure which is death.
I pray that I may die with ears wide open
to words of love spoken in my presence.
I pray that I may die with heart wide open
to the glorious promise of eternal love

To Brigid of Ireland

A Bhríd, a Mhuire na nGael,
may the warmth of your healing
surround me,
may the light of your faith
sparkle within me.
May the stillness of your spirit
descend upon me.
May the abundance of your generosity
abound in me.
When my time comes
wrap me in the folds of your cloak
and carry me with you to Tír na nÓg –
go dtí an tír ina mbíonn sé ina shamhradh i gcónaí.
[And carry me with you to the Land of Youth,
to the place where it is summer always.]

Into the arms of the Waiting One

I surrender into the heart of Love.
I surrender into the heart of Mystery.
I surrender into the heart of Silence.
O Radiant Light,
O Holder of my Dreams,
O God of Mystery,
lead me on paths of adventure
into ecstasy,
into beauty beyond my understanding,
into love beyond my wildest dreams,
into language for which there are no words,
into song that echoes through the vaults of time,
into music that transports me to places unimagin-
able.

Prayer to your guardian angel

O Angel of God, my guardian dear,
to whom God's love commits me here,
ever this day be at my side
to light and guard,
to rule and guide. Amen

Litanies

When old words die out
on the tongue,
new melodies break forth
from the heart.
And where the old tracks
are lost
new country is revealed
with its wonders.

Tagore

Litany: *Deep Peace*

Response, alternately:
Descend upon us
Arise within us

Deep peace of the flowing stream,
Deep peace of the gentle breeze,
Deep peace of the gliding swan,
Deep peace of the mighty oak,
Deep peace of the falling snow,
Deep peace of the tranquil forest,
Deep peace of eventide,
Deep peace of the still small hours,
Deep peace of the night sky,
Deep peace of the smiling moon,
Deep peace of the twinkling stars,
Deep peace of the quiet earth,
Deep peace of the silent rock,
Deep peace of the lapping wave,
Deep peace of the homing bird,
Deep peace of the hushed hedgerow,
Deep peace of the hibernating hedgehog,
Deep peace of the sparkling dew,
Deep peace of the sleeping baby,
Deep peace of the quiet bog,
Deep peace of the Source of all peace,

Prayer

Deep peace of the flowing wave to you!
Deep peace of the growing earth to you!
Deep peace of the gentle air to you!
Deep peace of the Giver of peace to you!
Amen.

Litany of longing

Response:
You are my soul's desire,
I long for you

God of my living,
God of my dying,
God of my loving,
God of my sorrowing,
God of my illness,
Source of all that is,
My soul's desire,
Beauty of Beauties,
Wonder of Wonders,
Creative One,
Heartbeat of the universe,
Miracle of birth,
Holy One,
Gentle One,
Eternal One,
Unknowable One,
Alpha and Omega,
Source of our dreaming,
Origin of our loving,
Love beyond all telling,
Joy beyond our imaginings,
Peace beyond our understanding.

Prayer

As a deer yearns for running streams
So I long for you, my soul's desire.
Reveal your face to me
In the love and care of those around me
And in the beauty of nature that surrounds
me.
Amen.

Litany of Homecoming

Response:
Centre us in you, O God

Home is where the heart is,
Home is the ground of our being,
Home is the theatre of our birth,
Home is the light in the window,
Home is the hearth of belonging,
Home is the place of discovery,
Home is the intimacy of family,
Home is the hug of forgiveness,
Home is the table of shared food,
Home is the dance of children,
Home is the song of tolerance,
Home is the locus of acceptance,
Home is the kiss of peace,
Home is the shelter in the storm,
Home is the welcome that awaits us,
Home is the Centre of our being,
Home is earth under our feet,
Home is the stillness at the Centre,
    Call us inward,
    Call us into the silence,
    Call us into the centre,
    Call us into you,
    Bring us home.

Prayer

O Holy One,
heart of the home, you are the lure
calling us inward,
calling us onward,
calling us home!
Awaken in us a sense of adventure
as we follow the call to journey into you!
Amen

Litany of Freedom

Response:
Carry us on eagle's wings

When we dream new dreams,
When we imagine new possibilities,
When we see distant horizons,
When we catch sight of hidden treasure,
When we dare to believe in the impossible,
When we long to rise above the pettiness of life,
When we desire to break free of the chains that bind us,
When we seek to break out of the beliefs that constrain us,
When we desire to leave the relationships that cripple us,
When we risk speaking our truth,
When we hunger for the bread that nourishes,
When we thirst for the water that satisfies,
When we long to be our true selves,
When we hear the sound of distant drums,
When we yearn to be one with all living things,
When we long for connection with earth, our home,
When we claim the delights of freedom,

Prayer

Carry us on eagle's wings into the delight of freedom.
Awaken within us the excitement of being our true selves,
free of obligation and duty,
free of constraint and confinement.
Secure in our place in the universe,
may we know the majesty and freedom of the eagle's flight!
Amen.

Litany during Chemotherapy

Response:
Source of my being,
Surround me with your love!

When nausea overwhelms me,
When I am too weak to raise my head,
When I ache all over,
When my mouth is a mass of sores,
When my body is covered with rash,
When my hair falls out,
When my features grow distorted with toxins,
When the pain is too much to bear,
When the night seems endless,
When I am unable to pray,
When friends find me impossible to deal with,
When family do not understand,
When darkness overshadows me,
When I am put to the test,
When I fail to appreciate the care that surrounds me,
When words of comfort seem empty,
When I am in despair,
When I am most afraid,
When I feel alone and deserted.

Prayer

Mother of Creation,
you who carry the pain of the world in your heart,
help me to accept willingly
the share of pain that is entrusted to me.
Lead me gently from self-pity and bitterness
to acceptance and peace.
Amen

Litany of Healing

Warmth of the sun,
Refresh me,
Coolness of wind,
Restore me,
Stability of mountain,
Anchor me,
Fluidity of water,
Cleanse me,
Intensity of fire,
Refine me,
First rays of dawn,
Heal me,
Solidity of oak,
Shelter me,
Fragrance of flowers,
Envelop me,
Flight of sparrow,
Sooth me,
Playfulness of lambs,
Fill me with hope,
Rays of moonlight,
Comfort me,
Magic of colour,
Wrap me with in your cloak,
Wonder of waves,
Renew me,

Silence of stone,
Strengthen me,
Intimacy of touch,
Embrace me,
Delight of friendship,
Re-create me,
Joy of family,
Warm me,
Exuberance of children,
Energise me,
Wisdom of the elders,
Guide me,
The whole of creation,
Enwrap me with healing.

Prayer

I call on creation to surround me
with its healing properties.
May the food I eat
bring healing and renewal to my body.
May the beauty I contemplate
bring peace and stillness to my spirit.
May the thoughts I think
bring life and love into my being.
Amen.

Litany of the angels

Angel of courage,
Give me strength to face the new day,
Angel of healing,
Restore my drooping spirit,
Angel of beauty,
Be by my side as I walk beautifully on the earth,
Angel of delight,
Play with me,
Angel of compassion,
Fill me with tenderness,
Angel of light,
Guide me,
Angel of stillness,
Bring me into the silence,
Angel of springtime,
Awaken new growth within me,
Angel of suffering,
Help me to endure this season of pain,
Angel of the dawn,
Fill me with hope,
Angel of the journey,
Shorten the road for me,
Angel of forgiveness,
Bless me with peace,
Angel of joy,
Dance in my steps,

Angel of music,
Be the song on my lips,
Angel of birth,
Gift me with restoration,
Angel of freedom,
Carry me on your wings,
Angel of the sea,
Row me safely home,
My guardian angel,
Be by my side.

Prayer
I ask the angelic choirs
to weave a song of love around me.
May their song raise my drooping spirit,
and fill me with renewed energy and hope.
Amen

Litany of thanksgiving

Response:
We raise our hearts in gratitude

For the wonder of our being,
For the gift of our senses,
For the beauty that surrounds us,
For the transforming power of suffering,
For the blessing of memory,
For the richness of imagination,
For the restoration of sleep,
For the renewal of the seasons,
For the healing power of humour,
For peace of mind,
For the blessings of sunshine,
For the rotations of the planets,
For the appearance of the stars,
For the gifts hidden in the house of pain,
For the release of a burden shared,
For the hush of silence,
For the companionship of animals,
For the shelter of trees,
For the majesty of the sea,
For those who inspire us,
For those who challenge us,
For those who bring laughter into our lives,
For those who love us,

For those who think of us kindly,
For mysteries we do not understand.

Prayer
May I be open to
the transforming power of suffering,
and raise my heart in gratitude.
May I accept the blessings offered in my pain,
and raise my heart in gratitude.
Amen

Litany of wholesome people

I recommend that you include patron saints,
ancestors and those who you admire in this litany.

Response:
Be with us on our journey

Mary, mother of Jesus,
Joseph, man of faith,
Mary of Magdala, first witness to Jesus' resurrection,
Peter of Rome, Rock of Strength,
Bridget, Muire na nGael (Mary of Ireland),
Patrick, Patron of Ireland,
Hilda of Whitby, woman of courage
Columcille of Iona, man of prayer,
Teresa of Avila, leader and reformer,
John of the Cross, contemplative poet,
Catherine of Sienna, theologian and spiritual guide,
Rumi of India, poet and mystic,
Hildegard of Bingen, musician and mystic,
Meister Eckhart, spiritual writer,
Claire of Assisi, lover of beauty,
Francis of Assisi, lover of nature,
Dorothy Keziel, modern martyr,
Oscar Romero, campaigner for justice,
Teresa of Calcutta, champion of those living in poverty,
Theilhard de Chardin, scientist and visionary,

Our/my ancestors on whose shoulders I/we stand,
Our/my patron saints (names),

Prayer
As we walk in the footsteps
of those who inspire us
may their dreams animate us,
their love hearten us,
and their courage sustain us.
Amen.

Blessings
in times of illness

Dear soul, most lovely of created things,
you who long to know
the place where true love is.
In order to find it
and be united with the source
learn that you yourself
are the room in which Love dwells,
the nook, the secret place
in which Love hides.

John of the Cross

We usually bless one another but one may also bless oneself.
Change the pronouns as appropriate.

Blessing of Peace

May you be free from unnecessary worry and anxiety.
May you be free from disturbed states of mind.
May you be free from the paralysis of fear.
May you recognise the seeds of peace within yourself,
and nourish them with care and tenderness.
May the peace that surpasses all understanding,
take root and blossom within you.

For your hidden self to grow strong

Out of the infinite glory of God
may you have the power
for your hidden self to grow strong,
so that God may live in your heart through faith,
and then, planted in love and built on love,
you will with all the saints have strength to grasp
the breadth and the length, the height and the
depth, until, knowing the love of God,
which is beyond all knowledge,
you are filled with the utter fullness of God.
Ephesians 3: 16-19

Blessing of Healing

May the Divine Healer
awaken the energy of healing within you.
May the medicinal properties of herbs
restore you;
May the purity of water
refresh you;
May the minerals in your food
strengthen you;
May the warmth of the sun
renew you;
May the serenity of tranquil water
calm you;
May the colour of the hedgerow
delight you;
May the song of the birds
enchant you;
May the gift of healing be yours in abundance.

Blessing of Love

May the blessing of love be upon you!
May you be loved deeply.
May you be loved long.
May you know the kiss of a thousand welcomes –
the embrace of forgiveness and peace.

Blessing of Silence

May you be brought to the depths of silence,
to a place of profound stillness,
a place where thought, with its words and images, ceases.
Here may you experience
a peace that surpasses all understanding,
a love that surpasses all knowing,
a union that is incapable of separation or division.
At the centre of this sacred place
may you come to know the depth of your connection
with all creation in the sacred web of life.

Blessing of the Universe *(Chinook Psalter)*

Blessing of galaxies, blessing of stars:
great stars, small stars, red stars, blue ones.
Blessing of nebula, blessing of supernova,
planets, satellites, asteroids, comets.

Blessing of our sun and moon, blessing of our earth,
oceans, rivers, continents, mountain ranges.
Blessing of wind and cloud, blessing of rain,
fog bank, snowdrift, lightning and thunder.

> Bless the wisdom of the holy one above us.
> Bless the truth of the holy one beneath us.
> Bless the love of the holy one within us.

Blessing of green plants, blessing of forest:
cedar, douglas fir, swordfern, salal bush.
Blessing of fish and birds, blessing of mammals:
salmon, eagle, cougar and mountain goat.

May all humankind likewise offer blessing:
old woman, young woman, wise men and foolish.
Blessing of youthfulness, blessing of children.
big boys, little boys, big girls and little ones.

> Bless the wisdom of the holy one above us,
> Bless the truth of the holy one beneath us,
> Bless the love of the holy one within us.

Blessing of Acceptance

May the grace of acceptance
well up within you;
may it trickle into your pockets of resistance;
may it water desert areas,
and wash away barriers.
May it fill your being
with a wholehearted 'yes' to your illness,
and to whatever the future holds.
May the blessing of acceptance
be yours and yours in abundance.

Blessing of Forgiveness

May the God of forgiveness bless you
and bless you kindly.
May the forgiveness you offer yourself
be gentle and wholesome.
May the forgiveness you offer another
be generous and wholehearted.
May the forgiveness you offer yourself be lavish.
May the forgiveness you offer another be prodigal,
May all whom you may have harmed
touch you kindly with forgiveness,
and may you know the peace of true forgiveness.

Blessing of Abundance

May the Field of Plenty bestow its riches on you.
In your hour of need
may friends gather around your table.
In your hour of pain
may a chorus of thrushes sing outside your window.
In your hour of loneliness
may the laughter of children reach you.
In your hour of questioning
may the perfect answer knock on your door.
May abundance be yours,
full measure, pressed down and overflowing.

Blessing of Joy

May all that sings sing in me/us.
May all that dances dance in me/us.
May all that delights delight in me/us.
May all that laughs laugh in me/us.

Blessing of Courage

May the courage of the warrior be yours;
May the courage of the climber be yours;
May the courage of Jesus,
who lived fearlessly, and who died nobly
be yours and yours in abundance.

Blessing of Awareness

May your ears be open
to the stirring of the Spirit
in all that lives and moves.
May your eyes be open
to the wonder winking beneath the surface
of all that breathes and dances.
May your heart be open
to the flow of energy and healing
hidden in your pain.
May you be surprised by the beauty
being unwrapped before your eyes.
May you be enraptured by the love
being unfolded in your heart.
May you be spell bound by the music
hidden in the heart of all created things.

Blessing of Truth

May you have the courage
to look into the mirror of truth.
May you see your real self,
devoid of falseness and illusion.
May you discover who you really are –
a rare, majestic jewel –
sparkling in the sacred web of life.
May you come to know the wonder of your beauty,
the amazement of your potential, the mystery of your being!

Blessing of Compassion

May compassion find a home in your heart,
and shine brightly through your eyes.
May your compassion extend especially to yourself.
May you treat your frailty with gentleness,
and your failings with forgiveness.
May the God of Compassion
hold you gently in a tender embrace.

Blessing of Freedom

May you fly on eagle's wings
to rise above the constrictions
that confine you.
May you soar high,
unobstructed,
in a spacious sky
above the limitations of your illness.
May you follow the call of freedom
to break out of your prison of pain.
May you know the exhilaration of the eagle's flight.

Blessing of Beauty

May the beauty of the sunset encircle you
and the fragrance of lilac surround you.
May the majesty of the mountain inspire you
and the energy of the sea empower you.
May the colour of the primrose clothe you
and the delicacy of the daisy delight you.
May the vision of the landscape enchant you
and the sparkle of the dewdrop excite you.
May you live in beauty all the days of your life,
and when your time comes may you
walk gracefully across the threshold of eternity.

Blessing of Light

May the blessing of light be yours!
May the glow of the votive candle
be the prayer within you.
May the power of lightening
be the energy within you.
May the flicker of firelight
be the spark of delight within you.
May the first rays of dawn
be the hope of renewal within you.
May the blessing of light radiate from your heart.

Blessing of Patience

May the blessing of patience be with you.
May the patience of Job,
who endured excruciating suffering
with resignation and acceptance, be yours.
May the patience of the penguin,
who endures incredible hardship
in fostering new life, be yours!
May the patience of the pregnant woman,
awaiting the birth of her first-born, be yours.
May the patience of the lover,
awaiting the return of the beloved, be yours.
May the patience of the farmer,
awaiting the first growth of spring, be yours.
May patience bud and blossom in your heart.

Blessing of Wisdom

May the wisdom of the sage heighten your awareness.
May the wisdom of the crone sharpen your judgement.
May the wisdom of the ancestors
deepen your understanding.
May the wisdom of the earth increase your insight.
May the wisdom of the universe
expand your consciousness.
May Sophia, Mother of Wisdom,
in-form and in-spirit you.
May She delight and captivate you.
May She be your constant companion and guide.

Blessing of all beings

May all beings have happiness.
May all be free from sorrow.
May all never be separated
from the Sacred Happiness which is Sorrowless.
And may all live in equanimity,
without too much attachment and too much aversion,
and all live believing in the equality of all that lives.
Buddist Prayer

Hebrew Blessing

May God bless you and keep you.
May God's face shine on you and be gracious to you.
May God bring you peace.
Numbers 6:22

Blessing of St Brigid

I would like the angels of heaven to be among us.
I would like an abundance of peace.
I would like full vessels of charity.
I would like rich treasures of mercy.
I would like cheerfulness to preside over all.
I would like Jesus to be present.
I would like the three Marys of illustrious renown
to be with us.
I would like the friends of heaven
to be gathered around us from all parts.
I would like myself to be a prayer to God,
that if I should suffer distress,
God would bestow a good blessing on me.
I would like a great lake of beer for our God,
I would like to be watching heaven's family
drinking it through all eternity.

The Caim: Blessing for Protection

This is a prayer from the Celtic tradition. Our ancestors formed a circle of protection around themselves with their hands for each blessing.

The love of God within me/you.
The warmth of God around me/you.
The embrace of God surround me/you.

The healing of God within me/you.
The care of God around me/you.
The gentleness of God surround me/you.

The stillness of God within me/you.
The tranquillity of God around me/you.
The peace of God surround me/you.

Blessing of St Patrick

Today in this fateful hour
I place all heaven with its power,
and the sun with its brightness,
and the snow with its whiteness,
and fire with all the strength it has,
and lightning with its rapid wrath,
and the winds with their swiftness along the path,
and the sea with its deepness,
and the earth with its starkness,
all these I place
by God's help and grace,
between myself and the powers of darkness.

I rise today through the strength of heaven,
light of sun,
radiance of moon,
splendour of fire,
speed of lightning,
swiftness of wind,
depth of sea,
stability of earth,
firmness of rock.

I arise today, through a mighty strength,
the invocation of the Trinity,
through belief in the threeness,
through confession of the oneness
of the Creator of Creation.

Blessing of angels

May the angels weave a circle of light around you
and shelter you in the shadow of their wings.
May they whisper words of comfort in your ear,
and sing songs of love in your heart.

When you walk through the valley of darkness
may the angels guide and protect you.
When you come to the door of death
may they carry you gently over its threshold.

Blessing of peace at night-time

May the peace of the quiet hours
gather you inward.
 May the hush of twilight
calm your spirit.
May the contentment of the homing pigeon
rest on you.
May the lapping of lake water
lull your soul to sleep.
May deep peace descend on you
and remain with you forever.

Blessings
for a happy death

We are encircled
By the arms
Of the mystery
Of God.

Hildegarde of Bingen

God of birth and death

God of the morning,
God of the dawning,
God awakening,
God beckoning,
God of each new day,
bless my life as it ebbs away.

Blessing for those who care for me

A blessing of kindness
on those who are sensitive to my pain.
A blessing of understanding
on those who are tolerant of my brokenness.
A blessing of peace for those who offer healing words.
A blessing of contemplation
on those who are careful not to intrude on my privacy.
A blessing of rapture
on those who shorten my day with story telling.
A blessing of fulfilment
on those who feed and nourish me.
A blessing of healing hands
on those who nurse and care for me.
A blessing of joy on all those who nurture and sustain me.
And a special blessing of love
on those who make my last days easier.

Blessing of Surrender

May your letting go be as tentative
as the fledgling's flight,
and as trusting
as the snowdrop's push through the clay.
May it be as gentle
as the falling of an autumn leaf,
and as gracious
as the melting of winter snow.
Above all, may it be as surprising
as a butterfly's emergence from its cocoon.

The blessing of death

May your letting go be gentle,
and your act of surrender full of grace.
May the stripping away be as painless as possible,
and the movement from death to new life
vibrant with promise.
May family and friends be at your bedside.
May the angels come to meet you.
May your ancestors
form a guard of honour by your side.
May Glorious Light beckon you onwards
into the folds of a loving embrace.

An old Celtic blessing

May the blessing of light be on you,
light without and light within.
May the blessed sunshine shine on you
and warm you heart till it glows like a great peat fire,
so that the stranger may come
and warm himself/herself at it,
and also a friend.
And may the light shine out of the two eyes of you,
like a candle set in the two windows of a house,
bidding the wanderer come in out of the storm;
and may the blessings of rain be on you –
the soft, sweet rain.
May it fall upon your spirit
so that all the little flowers may spring up
and shed their sweetness on the air.
And may the blessing of the Great Rains be on you,
may they beat upon your spirit
and wash it fair and clean,
and leave there many a shining pool
where the blue of heaven shines,
and sometimes a star.
And may the blessing of the earth be on you –
the great round earth;
may you ever have a kindly greeting
for those you pass as you're going the roads.
May the earth be soft under you when you rest upon it,
tired at the end of a day,

and may it rest easy over you
when at the last, you lay out under it;
may it rest so lightly over you
that your soul may be off under it
quickly and up and off, on its way to God.
And now may God bless you and bless you kindly.

Blessing for a journey

> May the way be smooth before you,
> and the wind on your back.
> May your companions shorten the road
> with tales of adventure and romance.
> May the inclines be gradual
> and the stumbling blocks few.
> May the signposts point homeward,
> and may there be an Irish welcome –
> The welcome of all welcomes –
> At journey's end.

Meditations

At the heart of contemplative living
is a re-engagement with awe.
Awe enables us to recognise
the connectedness of all things
and live in the humility
that flows from knowing
how connected we are.

Judy Cannato, *Radical Amazement*

Morning meditation

In that wonder time just before dawn,
as you gradually awaken
lie still and listen to the sounds of morning.
Dawn whispers in the distance.
The door of a new day is about to open.
Darkness yields to light.
Morning breaks.
The first rays of glory appear on the horizon.
Birds begin to sing:
listen to their song and take it into your heart.
Flowers open.
Leaves stir.
Animals open their eyes.
Humans stretch and yawn.
The sun rises golden, and yellow, and red, and orange.
Sunbeams dance on dewdrops.
In your mind's eye see dewdrops
glisten with the colours of the rainbow.
Turn your face towards the sun.
Feel its warmth on your face and on your entire body.
Cloth yourself in sunshine.
The new day dawns ablaze with splendour,
fresh with surprise, vibrant with promise.
Ask that your day be beautiful with light and colour.
Open wide your heart
and welcome the new day with gladness.
Arise full of hope determined to live this day to the full.

Meditation/Visualisation for Energy

Sit or lie in a comfortable, warm, quiet place.
Relax your body and your mind by breathing deeply.

Imagine you are in a red rose garden
on a clear sunny summer's day.
There are red roses all over the garden.
Their perfume fills the air.
Breathe in their scent as you admire their beauty.
In the centre of the garden
you see a patch of grass covered in red rose petals.
Lie down on the bed of red petals.
Red rose branches form a canopy over you.
Relax, surrounded by the scent of roses.
Feel the energy from the red roses entering into your body.
The energy flows into your heels and feet,
into your legs, into your buttocks,
into your abdomen, into your waist,
into your lungs and chest,
into your heart, into your shoulders,
into your hands and arms,
into you neck and head,
into your entire body.
Relax as energy fills your whole being.
Stay with this sensation for a few minutes.

At the end of the exercise your legs and feet will feel warm and
energised and you will experience more energy in your entire body.

Peace meditation

Lie or sit in a comfortable position. Focus on your breathing.
Breathe a little more slowly and deeply.

As you exhale, breathe out all negative thoughts and feelings.
Breathe in feelings of peace and well being.
As the air enters your body feel divine energy
circulating through your entire being
awakening each cell in your body.
Feel its power within you.
Feel its glowing light within you.
Relax in the joy and peace of this light.
Experience your entire being
glowing with light and with peace.
Send rays of this peaceful light
to each member of your family.
Send rays of light to all those whom you love.
Send rays of light to your neighbours and friends.
Send rays of light to people whom you find difficult.
Send rays of light to people who are ill or dying.
Send rays of light to war torn areas of the world.
Direct light and peace to all living creatures.
Spread light and peace all around the world.
Relax in the glow this light.

When you are ready return to normal awareness.

Meditation on the release of pain

This simple meditation may be used to help to alleviate one or more areas of pain. Sit or lie in a comfortable position. Settle into this position Become aware of your body. Close your eyes and breathe deeply and slowly.

Become aware of an area of pain
or discomfort in your body.
Focus your attention on that area.
Allow yourself to feel the pain and the discomfort.
Stay with the pain.
Feel its intensity.
Become aware of fear associated with the pain.
Stay with the fear.
Tighten the muscles around that area.
Feel the sensation of tightening like the tightening of a fist.
Slowly and gradually relax the muscles around the area.
Feel the sensation of softening.
Feel the sensation of letting go of the pain.
Release the pain.
Release the fear.
Relax your entire body.
Fill yourself with sensations of peace and wellbeing.

When you are ready, open your eyes and become present to your surroundings.

Relaxation Meditation/Visualisation

Lie down in a comfortable position.
Close your eyes. Focus on your breathing.
Breathe a little more slowly and a little more deeply.

Imagine that you are lying on a beach
on a beautiful sunny day.
Feel the warmth of the sun on your body.
Feel the warm sand under you.
Look up at the blue sky with its fluffy, white clouds.
Listen to the song of the gulls circling the shore.
Hear the waves break on the shoreline.
The tide is moving inwards.
The water comes to your toes.
It is cold and your body contracts
in a shiver as the wave recedes.
The next wave covers your feet.
The water is cold but it feels refreshing.
It washes away all the tension and stress
which has collected in your feet.
As the water recedes
your feet begin to relax and to feel heavy.
The next wave washes over your legs up to your knees
touching them with a healing touch.
As the water recedes it takes with it
all the tension from your legs.
A third wave comes over your thighs and abdomen.

The muscles and organs
of your thighs and abdomen contract;
relax as the water takes away all the tension
collected in these areas.
The fourth wave comes over your chest and arms.
As the wave recedes it takes with it
the stress lodged in those areas.
The muscles of your chest and your arms relax.
The last wave very quickly covers your whole body
and quickly recedes.
This wave takes with it
stress and tension from your face and head.
As it recedes you feel purified and clean all over.
Feel the sensation of being completely refreshed and clean.
Thank the water for refreshing and cleansing you.

When you are ready, open your eyes and stand up
filled with new energy.

Meditation/Visualisation on release of burdens

This meditation may be used to help to rid oneself of guilt,
lack of forgiveness, hurt, or bitterness. If you are well enough
it can be done on a river bank as a ritual.
Sit or lie in a comfortable, relaxed position.
Close your eyes and breathe deeply and slowly.

In your mind's eye imagine
that you are sitting beside a flowing river.
A row of trees
– sycamore, ash, chestnut, beach, birch, oak –
lines the river bank where you are sitting.
Woodlands line the opposite bank of the river.
Behind the woodlands a mountain range rises.
The water flows gently downward to the sea.
Two magnificent swans with their seven cygnets float by.
The trees are ablaze with autumn colour –
red, orange, yellow, and golden.
Notice that some leaves are falling into the water.
Watch them floating downstream on the water.
The trees have let go of their decaying leaves
so that new growth can bud in the spring.
Is it time for you to let go
of some of the burdens you are carrying
so that new growth can come into your life.
Become aware of some of the burdens
you are holding on to
– burdens that are weighing you down.

Be present to your heaviest burden
– of guilt, of hurt, of lack of forgiveness,
or of bitterness or whatever.
When you are ready to let go, pick up a leaf
and let it carry your burden downstream.
Watch it flowing on the water to the sea.
Feel yourself becoming less burdened:
feel a weight lifted from your heart.
The water now carries your burden.
Feel the joy of letting go.
Stay with this sensation of joy for a few moments.

*When you are ready, thank the water for taking your burden
and return to normal awareness.*

Meditation on grieving

You may need to use the pause button on your player often during this meditation. Sit in a relaxed, comfortable position.

With your thumbs explore the sensitive spot
between the breasts on your breast bone.
Allow your attention to come to the centre of the chest,
to the heart centre,
and feel the sensation right under the breast bone.
Is there a heaviness there? Is there a noticeable ache there?
Begin to press into that sensitive area.
Feel how the pain pushes back against the thumbs.
Experience the pain. Breathe into it.
Go deeper. Don't try to protect the heart.
Feel all the suffering and all the sorrow
of a lifetime's losses held there.
Feel the loss of connection with the natural world, our home.
Surrender to whatever feelings surface. Don't be afraid.
Open to the deepest grief held there. Experience this grief.
Place your right hand on your heart and feel the pain there.
Now breathe into the centre of the heart pain.
If tears come, allow them to flow.
Let them wash away your pain.
Allow awareness to penetrate
into the very centre of your being. *(Pause)*

Place your hands on your lap.
Breathe gently into your heart,
letting go of pain as you breathe out.

When you are ready open your eyes.
Adapted from Stephen Levine: Who Dies? An Investigation of
Conscious Living and Conscious Dying.

Night-time meditation

Lie down on your bed.
Close your eyes.
Breathe deeply and slowly,
letting go of the cares and worries of the day.
Become aware of the sensations of night time.
The last rays of the sun have sunk beneath the horizon.
Birds return to the trees
and tuck their heads under their wings.
Domestic animals curl up in baskets and kennels.
Farm animals lie down to sleep.
Flowers close their petals.
This is the time when the indigo cloak of night
enfolds all within its tranquil energy.
Feel yourself surrounded by a beautiful indigo cloak.
Safe and secure,
let go of all the cares and worries of the day.
Give thanks for all the blessings of the day just past.
Curl up in your indigo cloak.
Relax into a restful, peaceful sleep.

Rituals
in times of illness

Eternal life is reachable
Right here,
where I am,
Because eternal life
is life in
and with God,
And God is
where I am here
and now.

Henri Nouwen, *Here and Now*

*These simple rituals can be celebrated by yourself
or with a friend. Change the pronouns as appropriate.*

Be with nature

If you able, go outside each day for few minutes.
Be present to the earth, the great healer,
in all or any of the following ways.

Feel the wind on your face.
Walk on the grass.
Feel the warmth of the sun.
Listen to the song of the birds.
Put your hands in soil.
Cuddle a pet.
Walk on a beach.
Listen to a flowing stream.

Morning Ritual

Face the East.
Raise your arms in gratitude for the new day.
Take in the energy of the sun into your heart.
Encircle yourself with the sun's energy
by making a circle with your hands around yourself.
Breathe in the morning air
and feel yourself filled with its energy.
Reach down and draw up
the energy of the earth into your body.
Offer a prayer of gratitude for the new day
and ask for protection and healing.

Lighting a Candle

Materials needed: A candle, a candle holder and matches.

*Light the candle and say the following prayer
or one you compose yourself.*

Prayer
May I glow with the warmth of God's love today!

Blessing with Water

*Material needed: Water in a bowl and a sprinkler.
Use water from a local holy well, or any unpolluted water.*

Prayer
May this sacred water fall gently on me;
May its purity wash away all forms of negativity;
May its healing power calm and refresh me;
May its energy fill my being.

Rital of self-forgiveness

Place your hand on your heart.

Prayer
I ask forgiveness of myself
for failing to believe in my unique value.
I ask forgiveness of myself
for the times I failed to love and care for myself.
I ask forgiveness of myself for the things I have left undone.
I ask forgiveness of myself for the times I hurt others.
I ask forgiveness of myself for the times
I failed to appreciate the wonder and beauty of life.
I ask forgiveness of myself for the times …
(mention other times for which you need forgiveness)

*Bring your hands to the top of your head and slowly bring
them downward over your body in wiping gestures. Spread
your hands downward to the floor.*

Prayer
I wipe away all guilt, all shame, all regret from my being.

*Raise your hands upward and bring down the energy of the
Divine over your whole body,*

Prayer
May the healing energy
of the One who pulsates through all creation
fill my being with forgiveness, acceptance and love.

Sevenfold blessing

From the east – a blessing of hope and renewal
Face the east and draw this blessing into yourself
From the south – a blessing of acceptance
Face the south and draw this blessing into yourself
From the west – a blessing of wisdom and peace
Face the west and draw in this blessing
From the north – a blessing of courage and endurance
Face the north and draw in this blessing
From the rain – a blessing of refreshment and growth
Face upwards to the sky and draw down this blessing
From the sun – a blessing of energy and healing
Feel the sun on your face and breathe in this blessing
From the soil – a blessing of health and wholeness
Feel the ground under you and draw up this blessing

Blessing of hands

Materials needed: Hand cream, or an aromatherapy oil with soothing, calming properties, e.g. lavender, rose, camomile, geranium. These oils should not be applied directly to the skin but should be mixed in a carrier oil e.g. rape seed oil.
In this ritual I recommend that a friend massage each of the sick person's hands with hand cream or healing oil.

Prayer
Blessed be these hands that have nurtured life.
Blessed be these hands
that have given themselves to others in love and friendship.
Blessed be these hands that have held and comforted others.
Blessed be these hands that have toiled for others.
Blessed be these hands that have planted and sown.
Blessed be these hands that have known pain.
Blessed be these hands
that have woven beauty in many forms.
Blessed be these hands
that have sometimes been raised in anger.
Blessed be these hands
that have become toil worn and knotted with age.
Blessed be the Holy, Creative One
who formed these hands in your mother's womb.
Amen

Ritual of giving away

In this simple ritual it is recommended that you give away a treasured possession. This gesture is symbolic of ridding oneself of possessions and attitudes which do not serve you at this time.

Prayer
I give away this ..., a treasure that I have valued dearly.
May the person who receives it
be blessed with health and happiness.
May this gesture help to release my tight control of life
and free me of attachment to material belongings.
May it free me of attitudes or beliefs
that no longer serve my life's purpose.
May I trust in the abundance of a prodigal God
to supply what is necessary for me today.
Amen.

Ritual of Forgiveness

Prayer
Place your right hand on your heart and bring in outward in
a gesture of forgiveness.
If anyone has hurt me or harmed me,
knowingly or unknowingly, I freely forgive them.

Place your right hand on your heart and bow your head.
I ask forgiveness
if I have hurt anyone or harmed anyone,
knowingly or unknowingly.

Put your right hand on your heart and then stretch it
downwards towards the ground in a gesture of asking
the earth and its creatures for forgiveness.
I ask forgiveness of the earth
and of any creature that I have harmed,
knowingly or unknowingly.
May I be peaceful and free.
May my family and friends be peaceful and free. May my
enemies be peaceful and free.
May all creatures be peaceful and free.

Ritual with a shell

Theme: Secrets
Materials needed: A fairly large shell in which you can hear
the sea. Put the shell to your ear and listen to its secrets.

Reflection
The shell has many secrets:
Secrets formed on the ocean bed million of years ago,
Secrets of species that have long since become extinct,
Secrets of fishes
that have never told their story to anyone else.
What secrets do you hear?
Now bring the shell to your mouth and tell it your secrets.

Reflection
You have many secrets:
Secrets that you have never told another,
Secrets too deep for words,
Secrets that you want only the sea to hear,
Secrets about your feelings round your illness.
Thank the shell for listening to you
and ask it to hold your secrets close to its heart.

Letter Writing

This exercise can take a number of forms: letters of love and appreciation, letters of forgiveness, letters of asking for forgiveness, letters of gratitude etc.

Write a letter to people you love,
telling them how much you value their love.
Write letters of forgiveness
to those who may have hurt or harmed you.
Write letters asking forgiveness
of those whom you may have hurt, or harmed in any way.
Write letters of thanksgiving
to those who have helped and supported you.
Write to people who have been an inspiration to you.
Write to the earth and its creatures
thanking them for nourishing and supporting you.

Psalm Prayers

The only things
That count in life
Are the imprints of
LOVE
Which we leave
Behind us
After we are gone.

Albert Schweiter

For stillness

Response:
Be still, my soul,
and know the God within.

Centre me in your stillness;
Guide me into the silence.
Response

Lead me to the depth of my being;
Lead me to the depth of your love.
Response

Calm the tumult in my spirit;
Still the voices in my head.
Response

Quieten the torment in my heart;
Fill my being with your peace.
Response

Do not be afraid

(on Download)

> Response:
> *Eye has not seen,*
> *ear has not heard*
> *the depth of delight*
> *in the heart of our God.*
>
> Do not be afraid
> I am in you
> You are in me
> Do not be afraid
>
> Do not be afraid
> I am in the stars
> I'm hidden in the rain
> Do not be afraid
>
> Do not be afraid
> I am in the seed
> In the glow of the flame
> Do not be afraid
>
> Do not be afraid
> I am in all
> All in my embrace
> Do not be afraid

In times of suffering

Response:
Out of the depths I cry to you,
O God, hear my cry.

O God, My God,
to you I stretch out my hands,
to you I cry for help
in the lonely watches of the night!
Response

Suffering overwhelms me.
My body is in sore distress.
I am overcome with anxiety.
I am crushed and broken.
Response

I long for your healing touch.
I long for inner peace.
Source of my being,
 awaken your love and peace within me.
Response

God is my shepherd

Response:
O God, you are my shepherd
There is nothing I shall want

O God, you are my shepherd,
There is nothing I shall want.
In green pastures you give me repose,
beside restful waters you lead me.
You refresh my spirit.

You guide me along the right path.
You are true to your name.
Even though I walk in the valley of darkness,
I fear no evil, for you are at my side.
Your rod and your staff give me strength.

Goodness and kindness follow me
all the days of my life.
Based on Psalm 23

Psalm 139: God's presence

Response:
Where could I go from your spirit?
Where could I flee from your presence?

O God, you search me and know me.
You know if I am standing or sitting.
You perceive my thoughts from far away.
Whether I walk or lie down, you are watching;
you are familiar with all my ways.

Before a word is even on my tongue, O God,
you know it completely.
Close behind and close in front you hem me in,
shielding me with your hand.
Such knowledge is beyond my understanding,
too high beyond my reach!

Where could I go from your spirit?
Where could I flee from your presence?
If I climb to the heavens you are there;
if I flew to the point of sunrise –
or far across the sea –
your hand would still be guiding me,
your right hand holding me!

If I asked darkness to cover me
and light to become night around me,
that darkness would not be dark to you;
night would shine as the day.
You created my inmost being
and knit me together in my mother's womb.

For all these mysteries –
for the wonder of myself,
for the wonder of your works –
I thank you.

You know me through and through.
You watched my bones take shape
when I was being formed in secret,
woven together in the womb!
O God, your ways are mysterious!

God is my rock

Response:
Your steadfast love endures forever.

O God, my God, you are my rock,
the ground of my being.
Response

Mystery of molten lava,
your love is solid as stone.
Response

Majesty of mountain heights,
your promises are firm and constant.
Response

Your love is stronger than death,
your love endures forever.
Response

Fashioned in loveliness
(on Download)

Response:
You hold us in the palm of your hand.

Long before earth time emerges
Long before the spark of first dawn
Long before a cosmos unfolds
Long before galaxies are born
Long before, long, long before
You are dreaming me/us

Long before planets twirl in space
Long before life breathes in the sea
Long before flowers carpet earth
Long before insects come to be
Long before, long, long before
You are dreaming us/me

Long before sky bursts into song
Long before lions roam the earth
Long before mountains are formed
Long before humans come to birth
Long before, long, long before
You are dreaming us/me

Thanksgiving

Response:
We raise our hearts in gratitude

For the grandeur of the new day;
for the gift of life offered afresh.
Response

For the majesty of our being;
for the beauty of our spirit.
Response

For family who hold us in their embrace;
for friends who walk the road with us.
Response

For gifts hidden in the heart of suffering;
for medicine that lessens our pain.
Response

During Chemotherapy/Radiotherapy

Response:
O God, my God, I am in sore distress.

My eyes are weary from weeping,
my body is bruised and broken.
Response
Nauseous and weak,
I am unable to lift my head.
Response

My mind is in turmoil,
my spirit is disturbed and agitated.
Response

I am sore distressed.
I lie awake in the watches of the night.
Response

Open my eyes to recognise
the seeds sprouting in this winter field.
Response

Open my heart to embrace
the gifts hidden in this pain.
Response

Psalm of praise

Response:
Let all creation praise our God.

Unable to sing, I call on all creation
to sing a song of thanksgiving
for the wonders of God's Beauty,
for the abundance of God's love.
Response

Let the heavens ring out with joy,
and earth echo with song.
Let the sea and all within it rejoice,
and the rivers clap their hands.
Response

Let the mountains declare a feast,
and the forests celebrate with fanfare.
Let the wild beasts roam free,
and tame animals return to the wilderness.
Response

Let the stars dance with joy,
and the sun somersault with delight.
Let the sound of rejoicing and praise
resound through all creation.
Response

Rituals as death approaches

God, I still have a great fear
as to the way my soul
will pass from my body.
Then God said to me:
'It shall be thus:
I will draw my breath
and your soul shall come to me
as a needle to a magnet.'

Mechthild of Magdeburg

Ritual as death approaches

Preparation:
Have oils prepared. Mix an aromatherapy oil e.g. lavender,
rosemary, in a carrier oil e.g. baby oil.
Bowl of water and sprinkler. Candle.
Download with chants

Opening Prayer
[Name], we gather around your bed
to accompany you on your journey.
In God we live and move and have our being.
In God we live and die and have our being.
We live and die surrounded by awesome mystery.
Let us be present to the mystery of this moment.

Chant
(on Download)
Spiral of Mystery,
Calling you/us inwards,
Calling you/us onwards,
Calling you/us home.

Spiral of Mystery,
Luring you/us inwards,
Luring you/us onwards,
Luring you/us home.

Spiral of Mystery,
Leading you/us inwards,
Leading you/us onwards,
Leading you/us home.

Lighting a candle.
If appropriate place the lighted candle
in the dying person's hand.
We light this candle as a symbol of our love.
May its radiance guide you gently
into the radiance of eternal light.
Amen

Calling by name
[Name], we know and love you by your name.
Your name will remain forever in our hearts.
Each person present is invited to touch the dying person and
call her/him by name, saying
[Name], I love you.

Blessing with water
Use pure water or water from a Holy Well.
The leader blesses the person with water.
If appropriate others may also bless the person with water.
May this water fall upon you gently.
May it cleanse and calm you.
Amen.

Blessing with oils
The leader blesses the person with oil on the forehead or hands.
May the fragrance of God's love enfold you!
Invite others to anoint the dying person with oil. Any part of
the body may be anointed e.g. the hands, the forehead.

Litany as death approaches
This litany is divided into five parts – choose how much of it
is appropriate to recite.

Response:
Be with her/him

Mother of Sorrows,
Guardian of Pain,
Friend of the Weary,
Holder of Tears,
Guide of the Stray,
Healer of Hearts,
Comfort of the Dying,
Companion of the Wayward,
Embrace of Forgiveness,
Handshake of Welcome.

Response:
Surround her/him with joy

Cradle of Dawn,
Threshold of Light,
Miracle of Morning,
Messenger of Hope,
Maiden of Delight,
Mother of Promise,
Awakener of Dreams,
Dance of Sunlight,
Birth of Springtime,
Midwife of Joy.

Response:
Enfold her/him in love

Silence of Twilight,
Evening Star,
Mantle of Darkness,
Kindler of Starlight,
Mystery of Moonlight,
Haven of Rest,
Treasury of Dreams,
Shrine of Sleep,
Womb of Renewal,
Queen of Peace.

Response:
Come to meet her/him

Queen of the Harvest,
Gatherer of our Sowing,
Companion on the Journey,
Traveller's Rest,
House of Stillness,
Sanctuary of Peace,
Centre of Silence,
Heart of Love,
Lure of our Longing,
Our Soul's Desire.

Response:
Surround her/him with peace

Mother of Mercy,
Mother of Compassion,
Mother of Peace,
Blessed Mother,
Mother most tender,
Mother most loving,
Mother most gentle,
Mother of the welcoming arms,
Mother of the loving embrace,
Our Mother.

Prayer
Breathe your last breath into God.
Breathe your last sigh into God.
Breathe your last breathe into the universe.
May angels carry you.
May your ancestors come to meet you.
May your loved ones take your hand.
May your guides greet you.
May profound joy be yours.
May deep peace be yours.
May eternal love be yours.
Amen

Chant
(on Download)
Say or sing the chant.
As s/he falls into this embrace,
shelter him/her softly
in the folding of your wing.
Shelter her/him.
Hold her/him.
Enfold her/him.

Prayer after death
May your spirit meander through the folds of time.
May your song echo through all creation.
May your breath mingle with the breath of living things.
May your heart pulsate with the Heart Beat of Love.
May you dance in God, the Eternal One, forever. Amen.

Chant
(on Download)
In you we live,
In you we die,
In you we dance forever.

Closing of the eyes
The leader gently closes the eyes of the dead person.
[Name], gentle one,
your eyes shone brightly with the love of God.
We reverently close those eyes now.
May they now open to the wonder and joy of eternity.
Amen.

Visiting the body

Blessing the person who has died
I recommend that there be a basket of blessings on a table near
the bed. These can be very simple like 'I bless you with the
blessing of love/peace/joy etc'. Alternatively angel cards or other
such blessings may be used. Visitors have the opportunity to take
a blessing and say it (or another blessing) aloud or silently:
[Name], I bless you with the blessing of love.

The Download of chants
I recommend that the Download be played softly in the back-
ground.

Candles
A lighted candle or candles on a table near the bed.

Blessing with water
Water and a sprinkler on the table and the following or
similar text written beside it.

> Deep peace of the gentle rain to you.
> Deep peace of the flowing wave to you.
> Deep peace of the incoming tide to you.
> Deep peace of the Weaver of Peace to you.
> *Old Celtic Blessing*

The wake

S/he whom we love
and lose
is no longer
where she was before.
S/he is now
wherever
we are.

St John Chrysostom

The Wake

Welcome
We come together this evening to console another
in our grief.
We gather also to remember [name],
our beloved [sister, father, etc].
We are in the presence of Mystery.
God's energising presence pulsates
through our vast and wonderful universe.
In God we live and move and have our being.
All around us we observe
the constant rhythm of dying and rising:
of birth followed by death, followed by new life.
We believe that death is not the end
but the continuation of the ebb and flow of existence.
We believe that life is changed not ended.
[Name] lived and loved in God.
God lived and loved in her/him.
In death s/he continues to live and love in God.

Chant
(on Download)
Play, sing or say the words of the chant.

> In you we live.
> In you we die.
> In you we dance forever.

Reading
Our dead live forever:
for them life is changed,
not ended.
They are in God
and God's arms surround them.
In God they dance forever.
Based on Wisdom 5:15-17

Pause for reflection

Chant
(on Download)

> Eye has not seen
> Ear has not heard
> The depth of delight
> In the heart of our God.

Prayers of thanksgiving

In [name] the Spirit of God,
the Spirit of Life,
the Spirit of Love,
came to visible expression in human form.
[Name] showed that Spirit
in the way s/he loved and laughed,
in the way s/he cried and sorrowed,
in the way s/he worked and prayed.
S/he especially expressed the Spirit of Love and Life
in the way s/he patiently endured
the suffering of her/his final illness.

The leader mentions attributes appropriate to the person e.g:
[Name], manifested God's love
in the way s/he cared for her children,
in the way s/he gave a helping hand to neighbours,
in the way s/he loved to dance,
in the way s/he cared for plants and flowers etc.
Leave space for others to mention attributes peculiar to the
dead person.
We are grateful that [Name] touched our lives
in such beautiful, loving ways.
In [Name], we touched and were touched
by the Spirit of Love and of Life.
In her/him the Spirit of Love and Life
danced for joy.
Amen

Sharing of memories

[Name], has left us with many memories,
memories which we will cherish always.
What memory do you wish to share?
Allow time for people to recall memories.

Prayer

In the rising of the sun and in its going down,
we will remember her/him.
In the glowing of the wind and in the chill of winter,
we will remember him/her.
In the opening of buds and in the rebirth of spring,
we will remember her/him.
In the blueness of the sky and in the warmth of summer,
we will remember her/him.
In the rustling of leaves and in the beauty of autumn,
we will remember her/him.
In the beginning of the year and when it ends,
we will remember her/him.
When we are weary and in need of strength,
we will remember her/him.
When we are lost and sick at heart,
we will remember her/him.
When we have joys we yearn to share,
we will remember her/him.
So long as we live, s/he too shall live,
for s/he is now a part of us,
as we will remember her/him. *(Jewish Prayer)*

Litany of lament

The lament or keening is an old Irish custom. Participants at the wake give expression to their grief through chanting a lament.

Response:
If possible chant and ,if not, say:
We lament and say/sing
Ochón is ochón ó

We lament [Name]'s leaving us.
Response
We lament that we can no longer see her/his smile.
Response
We lament that we will no longer hear her/his laughter.
Response
We lament that we will no longer know
the warmth of her/his physical presence.
Response
We lament the times that we failed to appreciate
his/her love in our lives.
Response
We lament the times we hurt or saddened her/him.
Response

Allow time for participants to mention things for which they lament.

With all whom s/he cherished and loved we lament.
With all whom s/he influenced in any way we lament.
With all who are grieving this night we lament.
With all who are dying unloved and uncared for
we lament.
With all who are unable to express their grief we lament.
With all other species
we lament and say/sing
Ochón, ochón, is ochón ó!

Chant

(on Download)
The radiance of God around you/us
The warmth of God around you/us
The splendour of God around you/us
The shield of God around you/us

The energy of God within you/us
The stillness of God within you/us
The wonder of God within you/us
The creativity of God within you/us

The light of God around you/us
The love of God around you/us
The healing of God around you/us
The strength of God around you/us

The breath of God within you
The peace of God within you
The gentleness of God within you
The dream of God within you

Closing Prayer

[Name] continues to live and love in God
in ways beyond our human understanding.
In her/his life the Breath of the Eternal One breathed.
In her/him the Light of Divinity sparkled.
In her/him the Spirit of God danced.
May s/he twirl and dance in the Eternal One forever.
May all that we loved about her/him
continue to find expression in the ways
we love one another
and in the way we are open
to whatever the future holds.

[Name], your love will remain forever in our hearts.
Wherever you are we will be forever.
We will continue to share our memories
as we share food together.

End with a prayer that was important to the person e.g.:
Our Father *or* Hail Mary

Funeral Texts

We cannot judge a biography by its length,
by the number of pages in it;
we must judge by the richness of the contents.
Sometimes the 'unfinisheds'
are among the most beautiful symphonies.
Victor Frankl

I was lifted up into the arms of God,
a God whom I had thought could not exist.
I knew then the 'Peace that surpasses all understanding':
that supreme joy,
that Knowledge of the Ultimate Truth,
that Absolute Ecstasy
which I cannot begin to describe.
There are no words for
the complete Love and Light which enveloped me.
Quotation from a Near Death Experience.

Now we see in a mirror, dimly,
but then we will see face to face.
Now I know only in part;
then I will know fully, even as I have been fully known.
And now faith, hope, and love abide, these three;
and the greatest of these is love.
1 Cor 13:12-13

Beloved, we are God's children now;
what we will be has not been revealed.
What we do know is this:
when God is revealed,
we will be like God,
for we will see God as God is.
1 John 3:2

No eye has seen,
nor ear heard,
nor the human heart conceived,
what God has prepared for those who love God –
these things God has revealed to us through the Spirit,
for the Spirit searches everything, even the depths of God.
1 Cor 2:9

We lost our best friend
God, she taught us to call you the giving one
and now you have shown yourself as the taking one,
in taking her from us.
She who was our light is gone,
It is all darkness with us now.

She brought us gold and silver,
not of coin but of goodness and love.

God, give us back love.
She brought us flowering vines and leafing plants
in the gardens of our hearts.
She awakened our desires for you.

God give us back desire.
She brought us fields flung with riotous blossoms,
as she showed us the multifaceted dimensions of your light.
Now our eyes are dim with tears.
The light of our light and of our fields is gone.

God give us back light.
She gave us the sweet violet, the blushing rose,
and the gleaming lily.
She showed us the beauty of the land
and of the landscape of the soul.
Now all is arid and weariness.

God give us back beauty.
She spoke to us in words of joy and challenge and truth.
She brightened our world with pleasure
as the moon gleams against the darkness.
She herself walked in truth and now all truth is gone.

God give us back truth.

'Mourning for Radegund of Poitiers'
from Mary T. Malone, Praying with the Women Mystics

Before the mountains were formed
or the earth was born,
you are God, without beginning or end.
A thousand years are like yesterday to you –
come and gone –
no more than a moment in the night.
Help us realise the shortness of life
that we may gain wisdom of heart.
Psalm 90 adapted

Say not in grief
'S/he is no more'
but live in thankfulness
that s/he was.
Hebrew Proverb

Inside this clay jug
Inside this clay jug there are canyons and pine mountains,
and the maker of canyons and pine mountains.
All seven oceans are inside, and hundreds of millions of stars.
The acid that tests gold is there, and the one who judges jewels.
And the music from the strings that no one touches,
 And the source of all water.

If you want the truth, I will tell you the truth:
Friend, listen: the God whom I love is inside.
Kabir

Love is what God is
Would you know God's meaning in this thing?
Learn it well: Love is God's meaning.
Who showed this to you? Love.
Why did God show you? Love.
Why did God show it to you? For love …
And I saw surely that before God made us
God loved us,
and this love has never slackened and never will.
And in this love,
God has done everything.
And in this love God has made all things profitable for us.
And in this love
Our life is everlasting.
Julian of Norwich, quoted in Mary T. Malone, Praying with the Women Mystics

When I die if you need to weep
cry for your brother or sister
walking the street beside you.
And when you need me put your arms around anyone
and give them what you need to give me.

I want to leave you something
Something better than words or sounds.

Look for me in the people I've known and loved
and if you cannot give me away
at least let me live in your eyes and not your mind.

You can love me most by letting hands touch hands,
by letting bodies touch bodies
and by letting go of children that need to be free.

Love doesn't die, people do.
So when all that's left of me is love
give me away.
Anonymous

On dying

You would know the secret of death.
But how shall you find it
unless you seek it in the heart of life?
If you would behold the spirit of death,
open your heart wide into the body of life,
for life and death are one,
even as the river and the sea are one.

In the depths of your hopes and desires
lies your silent knowledge of the beyond,
and like seas dreaming beneath the snow
your heart dreams of spring.

Trust your dreams.
For in them is hidden the gate to eternity.
For what is it to die but to stand naked in the wind
and to melt into the sun?
And what is it to cease breathing
but to free the breath from its restless tides,
that it may rise and expand and see God unencumbered?

Only when you drink from the river of silence
shall you indeed sing.
And when you have reached the mountain top,
then you will begin to climb.
And when the earth claims your limbs,
then you shall truly dance.
Kahlil Gibran, The Prophet

All that thy child's mind
Thinks as lost
I have kept for thee,
Arise, clasp my hand and come.
Francis Thomson, The Hound of Heaven

Chant 1

Spi - ral of mys - ter - y call - ing me in - ward,
Spi - ral of mys - ter - y lur - ing me in - ward,
Spi - ral of mys - ter - y lead - ing me in - ward,

call - ing me on - ward, call - ing me home.
lur - ing me on - ward, lur - ing me home.
lead - ing me on - ward, lead - ing me home.

Chant 2

In You we live, in You we die, in

You _____ we dance for e - ver.

Chant 3

Eye has not seen, ear has not heard the

depth of de - light in the heart of our God.

Chant 4

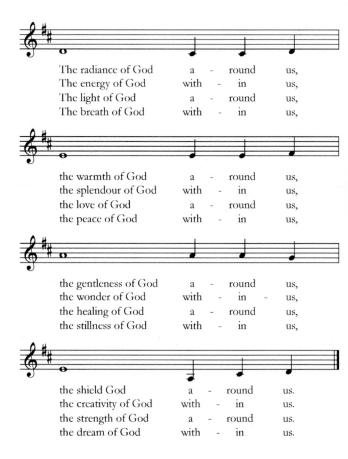

The radiance of God   a - round   us,
The energy of God   with - in   us,
The light of God   a - round   us,
The breath of God   with - in   us,

the warmth of God   a - round   us,
the splendour of God   with - in   us,
the love of God   a - round   us,
the peace of God   with - in   us,

the gentleness of God   a - round   us,
the wonder of God   with - in -   us,
the healing of God   a - round   us,
the stillness of God   with - in   us,

the shield God   a - round   us.
the creativity of God   with - in   us.
the strength of God   a - round   us.
the dream of God   with - in   us.

Chant 5

Long be - fore earth time e - mer - ges,
Long be - fore planets twirl in space,
Long be - fore sky bursts in - to song,

long before the spark of first dawn,
long before life breathes in the sea,
long before lions roam the earth,

long before a cos - mos un - folds,
long before flowers car - pet earth,
long before moun - tains are formed,

long before ga - lax - ies are born,
long before in - sects come to be,
long before hu - mans come to birth,

long a - go, long, long a - go,
long a - go, long, long a - go,
long a - go, long, long a - go,

You are dream - ing us.
You are dream - ing us.
You are dream - ing us.

147

Chant 6

Do not be a - fraid._____
Ná bíodh eag - la ort._____
Do not be a - fraid._____
Ná bíodh eag - la ort._____
Do not be a - fraid._____
Ná bíodh eag - la ort. Táim ag
Do not be a - fraid._____

I am in you,
Táim—se le do thaobh. Tá
I am in the stars.
Táim im - easc na réalta is sa
I am in the seed,
borradh ins an síol, is sa
I am in all,

you are in Me.
tusa im - o chroí.
I'm hidden in the rain.
bháis - teach bhog chaoin.
in the glow of the flame.
las - - air gheal bhuí.
all in my embrace.

Chant 7

Chant 8

Refrain

For those who walk the road with me,
lov - ers, __ dream - ers, fa - mi - ly, I
raise my heart in gra - ti - tude.

Verses

1. For tears and pain trans-form - ing me, for
2. For splen - dour wait - ing in each seed, for

care and love sus - tain - ing me, I
won - der wink - ing in each weed, I

To Refrain

raise my heart in gra - ti - tude.
raise my heart in gra - ti - tude.

Chant 9

As I fall in - to this em - brace shel - ter me soft - ly in the fold - ing of your wing. Shel - ter me, hold me, en - fold me. ____